THE FACE OF
TIBET

THE UNIVERSITY OF GEORGIA PRESS

ATHENS AND LONDON

THE FACE OF
TIBET

Photographs and Text by William R. Chapman

with a Foreword by His Holiness the Dalai Lama

The University of Georgia Press
gratefully acknowledges Marie-Anne Birken and REM
for their support in the publication
of this book.

*The author would like to thank Marie-Anne Birken for her
generous support and everlasting confidence in this project,
and Louise Gentry and Carol Craig for their help
with manuscript editing and encouragement.*

Published by the University of Georgia Press
Athens, Georgia 30602
Designed by Erin Kirk New
Set in Minion

*The paper in this book meets the guidelines for
permanence and durability of the Committee on
Production Guidelines for Book Longevity of the
Council on Library Resources.*

Printed and bound in Hong Kong
05   04   03   02   01   C   5   4   3   2   1

Library of Congress Cataloging-in-Publication Data
Chapman, William
*The face of Tibet / photographs and text by William R. Chapman,
with a foreword by His Holiness the Dalai Lama.*
p. cm.
ISBN 0-8203-2300-4 (alk. paper)
1. Tibet (China)—Pictorial Works. I. Title.
DS786 .C464 2001
951'.5—dc21   2001017153

British Library Cataloging-in-Publication Data available

The Face of Tibet is dedicated to Tibetans everywhere
and especially my dear friends and others living in Tibet
who endure a daily struggle to preserve and protect their way
of life. Their undaunted and compassionate courage
has always been an inspiration.

Contents

Foreword

His Holiness the Dalai Lama

Tibet is an ancient nation with a unique culture and civilization. Many people might attribute this solely to the profound influence of Buddhism, but I feel that the Tibetan character, and with it Tibetan civilization, has also been shaped by the unique land of Tibet. Surrounded by forbidding snowcapped mountains, our vast land is wide-open beneath the clear blue sky. The rolling grassy plains, too fragile to support agriculture, are ideally suited to a nomadic way of life—a happy and unconstrained existence. Even farming communities in the river valleys are fiercely independent in their self-sufficiency. Life in Tibet gives us a strong sense of freedom, both physical and spiritual, while the rigors of the climate have made us robust and resilient.

In recent years, the people of Tibet have needed these qualities like never before. A climate of oppression currently prevails in Tibet. Virtually everything of significance to Tibetans is under attack. In recent decades, hundreds of thousands of people have died, and thousands who have committed no crime other than patriotism have suffered years of imprisonment. Our monasteries and nunneries, the repositories of our rich and ancient culture, our sources of education, have been demolished. Our institutions of government have been set aside, so that the destiny of Tibet and its people is no longer in the hands of Tibetans. Our natural resources, which we used carefully and treated with respect, have been wantonly plundered and the environment spoiled. Even the wild animals that once lived without fear of human beings have been ruthlessly eliminated.

At the same time, the people of Tibet are almost powerless to respond. The Chinese authorities brook no opposition to their rule. Protest provokes an invariably harsh reaction. This is where we Tibetans who live in exile, and friends like the author of this book, have a special responsibility, for we have the freedom to speak up for our brothers and sisters in Tibet. We can now make known the reality of life in our homeland. We can help increase awareness of the value of Tibetan culture and the loss of humanity if it should be allowed to disappear.

This book contains photographs that Bill Chapman has taken in Tibet. They provide a vivid record of life in the Land of Snow, the beauty of the landscape, the distress of the Chinese occupation, and Tibetans' undiminished determination to regain what we have lost. We Tibetans may belong in a remote land, but like everyone else, we want to live in peace and happiness, and like everyone else, we have a right to do so. I hope readers whose interest is stirred by this book may also be inspired to give us their support to achieve these fundamental goals.

Preface

Tibet is a land and a place high above all others. A wild land of boundless space filled with overwhelming splendor and fierce desolation, where the daily routines of people's lives, religion, and spirituality are merged into one. A place that, until the 1950s, had been isolated from the outside world for hundreds of years. A land sometimes called the "Roof of the World."

For much of my life Tibet has been synonymous with adventure and mystery. Prompted by this image I decided to go there on a journey of personal and photographic discovery and exploration. The memory of Tibet's multiplicity of landscapes will, of course, always be beautiful and inspiring to me—such exotic, breathtaking views would leave a deep impression on anyone's memory. But the most vivid, significant memories were left by its people; the opportunity to become acquainted with and live among them—even for such a short time—has been one of the greatest experiences of my life. I was charmed, humbled, and deeply moved by the spirituality of these unique people and their abiding sense of humor and joy for life. The positive outlook they convey is all the more admirable considering the injustices and crimes of oppression they have endured during forty years of occupation by the Chinese.

A most unlikely part of my journey was meeting a young Buddhist monk whom I will simply call Yeshi. We met at a monastery in central Tibet. Yeshi and his family were on a pilgrimage to the various holy sites in that region. They invited me to join them for lunch at their campsite, and that encounter was the beginning of a friendship that forever changed my relationship to the people of Tibet. Though we spoke different languages, Yeshi and I quickly developed an intuitive understanding and trust that continued to grow during our time together.

In our subsequent travels, most of the areas to which Yeshi took me were closed to foreigners. They were "forbidden" places, and access to them allowed me the opportunity to become intimately acquainted with a side of Tibet that has rarely been seen or photographed by outsiders. Much of the inspiration for this book developed from that time and from the extraordinary bond that Yeshi and I share. That is why, at least to me, *The Face of Tibet* is much more than merely a collection of photographs.

Though there have been many changes in the political and social structure of Tibet over the past four decades, the will and faith of the Tibetan people remain undiminished. It is my hope that the images in this book will serve as a tribute to their tenacity, a display of visual beauty that penetrates the surface to take the reader to a more inward look at the very soul of this spiritual place and people.

THE FACE OF
TIBET

Introduction

The Plateau of Tibet is a vast geographical area covering more than 830,000 square miles, an area larger than western Europe or the state of Alaska. It is the highest and largest plateau in the world, with an average elevation of fifteen thousand feet. Because the land is composed of such wild and desolate spaces, many parts have never been trod upon by humankind, not even by native Tibetans.

Despite Tibet's isolation from much of the world, over the centuries Tibet's people had to contend with numerous political disputes with their nearest neighbors. Still, Tibet always asserted and maintained integrity as a sovereign nation. This age of solitary innocence was brutally changed in the 1950s as a result of the Chinese invasion and occupation of Tibet. Since that time, there has been a deliberate, aggressive program to destroy and suppress much of the culture, religion, and fabric of Tibetan life. During the Cultural Revolution in China, thousands of innocent people were imprisoned, persecuted, and killed because their beliefs and institutions differed from those of their oppressors. Untold numbers of Buddhist monks and nuns were tortured, killed, or banished from their home monasteries. Many of these monasteries were either damaged or destroyed during the same period. The huge influx of Han Chinese into the region caused an upheaval of traditional agricultural practices that resulted in unprecedented famine and starvation from 1959 to 1963 and again from 1968 to 1973. Religious expression of any kind was not tolerated, and contrary behavior was dealt with harshly.

Although these deliberate acts of brutality were among the most tragic in recent history against such an independent and passive country, the rest of the world proved unwilling to aid the defenseless Tibetan nation.

Conditions in Tibet have improved somewhat in the last two decades, albeit tenuously. Even Chinese officials were unable to ignore the deplorable effects of their occupation. Many of the failed policies they instituted were discarded or changed to restore economic stability. China has invested heavily in Tibet in recent years, helping to rebuild a freer market economy. Unfortunately, much of this investment and growth is directed to benefit and expand the Chinese presence and influence in the region.

Some would say the standard of living for Tibetans is higher now due to the influx of foreign goods and the building of roads and power plants. However, most of the "improvements" from the modern world came at a painfully high price and were neither needed nor sought by the average Tibetan. Outside influences would have eventually forced Tibet to come to terms with the realities of the modern world, but the people and government of this peaceful land were denied the liberty to accept change in their own way and time.

For the outside world, one of the most important reforms implemented by the Chinese is that since 1983 many of the barriers to tourism in Tibet have been relaxed. Individual travel remains strictly controlled, however, and is often hindered by frustrating and time-consuming dealings with the Chinese bureaucracy. Travel itself is neither easy nor comfortable in the modern sense, and the routes to many destinations remain difficult, dusty, tiring, and at times even dangerous. But visitors will find that despite the turbulent political and social changes that have occurred over the last few decades, many parts of the Tibetan landscape remain untouched and unchanged, and much of the traditional daily life continues as it has for countless generations.

The Mountains of the Plateau

Over two hundred million years ago, Tibet lay under the sea, and what we now call India was a large island thousands of miles to the south of where it is today. Over time this continent drifted north toward the Asian continent. A massive collision occurred between the two, and the northern edge of India slid under the Asian shelf. As it forced its way up and under the landmass, the Tibetan plateau and the Himalayan mountain range were slowly but steadily thrust up into the sky. This process continues today, as the great peaks of this range gain almost an inch a year in height.

North of these mountains is where Tibet begins. Traveling through this secluded country can be both inspiring and humbling. It is one of the few places where one can encounter pure silence. To stand alone, gazing toward an endless horizon, and not hear or see anything man-made is an unforgettable experience. I believe this singular silence, coupled with the simplicity of life for most of the people living here, contributes to a peacefulness and fulfillment rarely found elsewhere in the world.

A yak train carries supplies and gear to advanced base camp on Mount Everest.

Preceding page: A lone horse and cart *(lower left)* in the Mount Everest region.

The approach to the northern slopes of Mount Everest as seen from near base camp. Tibetans believe that with the fluttering of these flags, the prayers and mantras inscribed on them are released into the wind and carried throughout the world.

Preceding pages: An isolated dwelling in central Tibet.
In the springtime, ice remains in many high-altitude
streams as they make their way toward larger rivers.

Arid sand dunes
and landscape south
of Lhasa.

Under the ever-watchful eye of Mount Everest, also known as Chomolungma, Mother Goddess of the Earth, a farmer near the village of Tingri prepares a field for the sowing of barley.

The slopes of Mount Everest are the source of the pure, frigid waters that flow along the Rongphu glacier to the lower plateau and plains of Tibet.

Mount Everest from near Rongphu Monastery.

Prayer flags atop a high pass overlooking Lake Yamdrok in central Tibet.

Lhasa—The Forbidden City

For hundreds of years, the city of Lhasa tried to protect the purity of its culture by prohibiting outsiders from visiting without a special invitation. The fabled city still drew curious and dauntless adventurers from afar, but few succeeded in their quest. Even today, getting there by means other than air travel is an arduous trip. When at last the seeker catches the first view of the forbidden city of Lhasa, the sense of wonder and accomplishment intensifies to an emotional and almost magical experience.

Lhasa is a meaningful destination not only for foreign travelers, but also for Tibetans, many of whom stream into the city every day—some of them on religious pilgrimages, others merely going about the business of their daily lives. Even greater numbers converge upon the sacred city during special religious festivals. Whenever I return, I always experience the same feeling of awe upon seeing the Potala Palace standing sentinel above the sprawling city and surrounding countryside.

Anybody who visited Lhasa ten or twenty years ago would scarcely recognize much of the city today. Present-day Lhasa is dominated by the typical, bland architecture of the modern Chinese style. Spreading out from the foot of the Potala Palace is a new city of office buildings, storefronts, blaring karaoke bars, and everything else it takes to make the Chinese feel at home. The old Tibetan section of the city, though caught in the stranglehold of modern-day development, abounds with enduring evidence of Tibetan culture. It is here, in a city struggling desperately for its very life, that pilgrims walk the Barkhor circuit around the Jokhang Temple, the most sacred religious site in Tibet.

Tibetan children take time from thei
game for a group portrait near the
Jokhang Temple in Lhasa.

Preceding page: The spectacular Potala Palace dominates the
skyline in the center of Lhasa. Many successive incarnations of
the Dalai Lama ruled Tibet from the eleven-hundred-room
palace until 1959. This view is from the former site of the
College of Traditional Tibetan Medicine. The school was
destroyed shortly after the Chinese occupation of 1959.

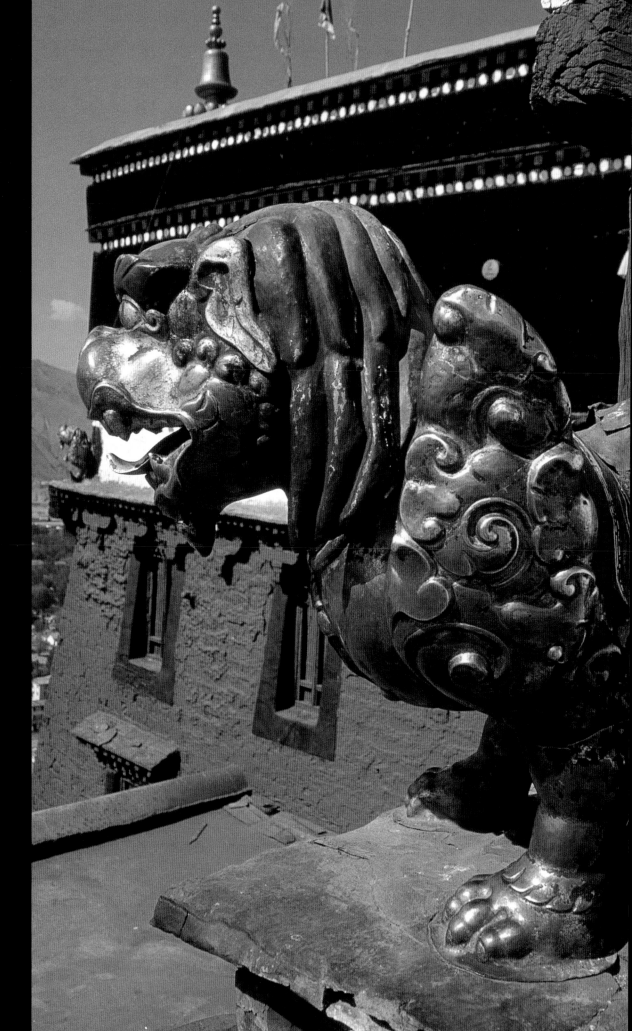

The Snow Lion, the
eternal symbol of
Tibet, watches over
Lhasa from atop the
Potala Palace,
protecting the city
against negative
spirits.

A Chinese military band packs up after a public performance across from the Potala. Seconds after this photo was taken, an officer ordered me to leave the scene.

Preceding pages: Towering Buddhist shrines, called *chortens,* stand at the ancient gateway to the Potala Palace.

A stone carving of Buddha reflects in a small lake outside Lhasa.

A Lhasa girl flashes a shy smile and a
hand sign that Tibetans use as a gesture
of peace and goodwill.

Potala Palace.

Bright colors in a Tibetan market. Peppers like these are used to flavor *thukpa* (Tibetan soup).

A pilgrim shops for a new prayer wheel at the Barkhor Market in Lhasa. Prayer wheels, which contain printed Buddhist religious text and mantras, are used throughout Tibet, and it is believed that each spin of the wheel represents a recitation of the prayers and brings blessings to the spinner.

This elderly woman, who once was a traditional Tibetan opera singer, has an ingenious prayer wheel that can be spun without being held.

A pilgrim makes an offering at an incense burner outside Jokhang Temple in Lhasa. Tibetans believe that their prayers and devotional words are transferred to the burning incense and then carried into the wind by the fragrant smoke.

A pilgrim visits Lhasa.

Life in the Country

Most of the people of rural Tibet are either farmers or nomads. The farmers live and work on the same land year-round, and the nomadic people roam the vast open plains, always in search of abundant grazing for their animals. Most farm families also tend livestock, but they generally confine their movements to within a few hours' walk of their homes. Farmers and nomads are harmoniously linked to each other through trade, religion, culture, and an ever-compelling need to produce the food to sustain their very existence.

The most important food source throughout Tibet is barley, and the most important food is *tsampa,* which is made by roasting whole barley grain in heated sand, then separating it and grinding it into flour. It is extremely common to see *tsampa* placed in a cup or leather bag, mixed with tea or milk whey, and kneaded by hand into a doughlike mixture called *pak.* Though *pak* is only one of the many foods made from *tsampa,* it is so well appreciated that few Tibetans would think of starting the day without it. Barley is also used to produce traditional Tibetan beer, called *chang;* yeast is added to the cooked and cooled grain and the mixture is stored in large jars for fermentation.

The yak, because it is the primary source of energy for plowing and farming, is crucial for the production of barley. But it also serves as another important source of food and other valuable materials. Its milk and milk-based products, such as butter and dried cheese, are highly regarded throughout Tibet. Every part of the yak is used in some way. The dried dung is a principal source of fuel, and the burned ash is used for fertilizer. The hides are dried and used for coverings, and the hair is woven into ropes, sacks, garments, blankets, and tents; the hair can even be compressed into felt for use in hats and handmade boots.

In Tibet, riding horses is a way of life and a source of excitement. Though most Tibetan horses are small in stature, they tend to be very tough and hardy.

Preceding page: The yak is the primary source of energy for agriculture in Tibet. During the plowing seasons, the delicate sound of yak bells resonates in the countryside.

A young girl heads home after delivering some grain that will be ground into flour.

The country mastiff. These dogs are usually kept on a leash that is tied to a large peg in the ground.

These giant mastiffs are not just for show; they take their guard duties seriously.

Two sisters share threshing duties on a
breezy afternoon. Mechanical harvesting and
threshing equipment is almost unheard of
in Tibet, even today.

Tibetans are very serious and
discriminating about the quality of
their *tsampa*. It is clear that weight is
not the only thing that these women
are considering as they examine the
tsampa at a local market.

A *tsampa* mill in central Tibet.

A mighty bull yak takes a rest as he keeps watch over his domain. Yaks are raised and kept by farmers and herders throughout Tibet and are highly revered and valued. These hardworking animals routinely are used to till the fields, to carry heavy loads (including people), and to provide milk for butter, yogurt, and cheese.

On a windy morning in
the grasslands region of
eastern Tibet, this young
woman and I did our
laundry in the same
running stream.

A grasslands woman pauses
after gathering wood for fuel.

A yak takes a rest from
pulling the plow.

A woman and child take their
turns with the plow. The division
of labor in eastern Tibet is not
based on gender, and it is
common to see women handling
teams in the field.

A woman shows off two of her favorite companions. Her donkeys are vital to her everyday life. In many ways, donkeys are hardier than horses, and they thrive under the hard conditions of life on the high plateau.

A farmer's wife in the highlands
of central Tibet.

A mother and daughter walk
across a field recently plowed in
preparation for sowing barley.

Wild blue sheep, known as *bharal*,
are found on rugged cliffs above the tree
line throughout the Tibetan plateau.

The Tsangpo River near the city of Shigatse.

An elderly woman waits for her
family members to return with their
herd of sheep.

Girls displaying their finest outfits at
an annual horse-riding festival in a
small village in the Mount Everest
region. This event draws many
participants from surrounding villages
for a celebration that continues late
into the night.

A young participant at a horse festival shows his determination during a competition on the course.

A festival goer shows off his fox-fur cap at a horse festival in south central Tibet.

The Children of Tibet

In this modern age, it is a remarkable thing to observe children away from the influences of television, video games, and other intrusions of today's world. There seems to be an innocence in the children of Tibet that carries on throughout their lives. Some of the most treasured moments from my many months and miles of travel in Tibet were chance encounters with the ever-delightful children. Their curiosity and enthusiasm were always welcomed and appreciated.

Preceding page: A girl looks after her two brothers
while touring the Jokhang Temple in Lhasa.

A young girl, standing at the Jokhang Temple in Lhasa, on a pilgrimage with her family. They have come a long way from their rural home far to the east.

These two young pilgrims have just completed a long day of doing devotional prostrations on the circumambulation route around Jokhang Temple in Lhasa.

American pop culture influences can be seen
in the most unlikely places, but these boys pay little
attention to the emblems on their caps.

A girl sells dried cheese in a small
village near Gyantse.

These young shepherds live in the desolate
region north of Nylam in central Tibet.
Their hardy flocks provide some of the
highest quality wool and cashmere in
the world.

Eastern Tibet, 1998, moments after a
school dance program.

Near Nylam in central Tibet. Family closeness and interdependence are important to those who grow up in an isolated area. Playmates are scarce, so siblings become attached to, and protective of, one another.

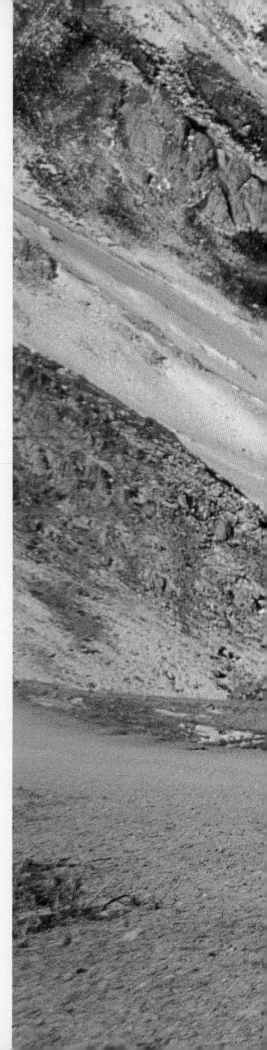

A young pilgrim on a lonely section
of road in south central Tibet.

Sisters. Children in many of the remote
areas seldom see strangers and are always
curious, if a little shy.

A young man who has just traveled several hours on the back of a truck, enduring dust and the high-altitude sun.

Preceding pages: Prayer wheels at Sera Monastery.

A curious girl on a
side street near the
Kumbum section of
the local monastery,
in the town of
Gyantse.

This young woman's family was planting a field of barley near a small village in central Tibet, and she stopped her work for a quick chat.

At a small monastery in the Amdo region, this young boy helps a crew of workers tamp down a new mud roof.

Monasteries and Pilgrimage

For centuries before the Chinese occupation, many young boys—approximately 20 percent of the male population—were raised in the monasteries of Tibet. Many young girls became nuns, although their numbers were not as high. More than six thousand monasteries scattered all over Tibet assured a young boy the opportunity to get an education, rise in the ranks, and possibly become a learned and important member of society, even if he had come from a poor or underprivileged family. Although life in a Tibetan monastery might be perceived by Westerners as dreary and somber, the atmosphere in the average monastery is characterized by inviting smiles, contagious laughter, shared brotherhood, and the uplifting feeling of being in a place where genuine spirituality lives.

Vast numbers of these monasteries were either destroyed or dismantled during the time of the Cultural Revolution, but today there is widespread rebuilding and renovation taking place. It is not unusual to see dozens of local Tibetan people working daily on the restoration effort. In many places, the work is being done with volunteer labor and Tibetan financial resources. To see people of all ages and abilities working together on this type of building project is inspiring. Most Tibetans hope that the restored monasteries will once again become theological colleges and centers for the artistic and religious culture of Tibet.

Because many monasteries are located near important religious sites, the act of pilgrimage is linked closely with them. A pilgrimage to a religious site is very different from ordinary travel. The focus of such a pilgrimage is more on what is gained along the way than on arrival at the destination. Buddhists believe that by undertaking these journeys, they will gain religious merit and hasten their personal growth.

A pilgrimage involves a great investment of time and determination, and the distance traveled can be both long and difficult. However, the mental and spiritual insights experienced during these long journeys, especially in the wide expanses of nature, are thought to add coherency and help shape a person's outlook about the future of his or her religious practice.

Two of my young friends rush to greet me on my return to Gomang Monastery in eastern Tibet.

Preceding page: A young monk during philosophical debates at a monastery in far-east Amdo.

Afternoon debates
at Sera Monastery.

Teacher and student in Gomang
Monastery. Mentoring is an integral
part of the monastery system.

Inside the Ganden Monastery near Lhasa, monks gather for morning prayer readings and chants.

A young pilgrim makes his way around the four-mile circumambulation circuit of Labrang Monastery in far-eastern Tibet. Devout Buddhists believe that they gain spiritual merit on these long and tiring journeys in a position of full prostration.

An old man makes his daily circumambulation route around Tashilunpo Monastery in Shigatse. Like others who follow the route, he walks in a clockwise direction, always keeping the rows of prayer wheels to his right.

At certain isolated monasteries in eastern Tibet, the prayer flags are displayed in a unique way.

Preceding pages: Labrang Monastery in far-eastern Tibet.

During their practice,
the dancers are
accompanied by this
small but effective band.

Preceding pages: Two monks move in unison during
dance practice at Labrang Monastery.

Gomang Monastery in eastern Tibet.

In the foreground is a sacred *chorten* destroyed by the Chinese
during the Cultural Revolution. Attempting to rescue the shrine
from destruction, three monks placed themselves atop it
and were killed in the explosive blast. In the background, a new
chorten is being built almost entirely with Tibetan labor and funds.
When completed, it will be the largest *chorten* in Tibet.

Resident monks work to rebuild a small monastery in Amdo, exemplifying the many restoration projects in progress all over Tibet. Though the Chinese in recent years have condoned much of the rebuilding, they continue to maintain tight control over the activities and membership of Tibetan monasteries.

Most of the restoration work taking
place today in Tibet is done by local
Tibetan volunteers.

Monks pray together before
beginning their debate exercises
at Gomang Monastery.

During a morning religious
debate at Gomang Monastery,
a young monk holds court
and emphasizes his position
by slapping his hands
together. These debates hone
the intellect of the young
trainees and prepare them for
future religious examinations.

One of my young friends at Gomang Monastery.

These young monks of Tsurpu Monastery in central Tibet are absorbed in their morning lessons in this monastic classroom.

During an afternoon debate in a courtyard
at Sera Monastery, a young monk listens
intently to the questions of an older mentor.

A monk makes his way
to the main assembly hall
in a small monastery in
central Tibet.

These nuns live in a small nunnery built among hillside caves in eastern Tibet. They share the duty of caring for an aged high lama nearby.

Old men enjoy the warmth of the afternoon sun at a pilgrim camp near Gomang Monastery in eastern Tibet. Note the assortment of prayer wheels in use.

Tsurpu Monastery in central Tibet was the seat of the Seventeenth Karmapa, leader of the Kyagyu school of Tibetan Buddhism, who recently fled to India.

Preceding pages: Persistence and motivation are represented by this elderly man as he performs *koras,* or circles, around a religious shrine near Labrang Monastery in far-eastern Tibet. It is not uncommon for pilgrims to perform hundreds of these circles around one structure to express a sense of virtue and gain *sonam,* or spiritual merit.

The Nomads of Amdo

Tibetans are born traders, and none more so than the wandering nomads of an area known as Amdo. In the past, some of these nomads were notorious for robbing other traders and travelers passing through their part of the country. To this day, the people of Amdo have a somewhat wily reputation left over from their ancestors. They also have a keen sense of style when it comes to clothing. The people of Amdo wear traditional Tibetan dress despite their proximity to China. The women, especially, like to adorn themselves in brightly colored garments, accented by ancestral-style jewelry. It is common to see a group of mounted riders driving a herd of yaks or tending sheep, sporting a splendid display of regalia.

When traveling through this tranquil land, which is in the green, rolling mountains of far-eastern Tibet, it is hard to imagine the hardships that its inhabitants have experienced during the past forty years. Perhaps because of their proximity to the Chinese border, the monasteries and nomadic herders in this region suffered particular devastation after the Chinese invasion of the 1950s. The large nomadic tribe known as the Goloks defiantly resisted the Chinese occupation for more than two decades, but their numbers were decimated by systematic massacres, starvation, and imprisonment that resulted in the deaths of untold thousands. Hundreds of the region's monasteries were damaged or destroyed, and most of the monks and nuns were banished from their homes.

Despite the deliberate attempt to change and remodel the way of life in Amdo after 1959, and despite the multitude of hardships that have existed since then, the tenacious spirit of frontier freedom still thrives within the people of Amdo today. Their enduring spirit is directly linked to the other people and regions of Tibet and their deep-seated commitment to Tibetan Buddhism.

Since the time of the Cultural Revolution, life and conditions here have gradually returned to a more traditional, settled state. The native Tibetans now enjoy a "freedom," but it is a freedom with definite limitations. Overshadowing their lives are the ever-present displays of power by the Chinese and the knowledge that the rules could change at any moment.

A woman from the grasslands
region of Amdo.

Preceding page: Horsewomen of Amdo,
dressed in native attire.

My traveling
companions pass a
chorten while visiting
a monastery in
eastern Tibet.

A mother and child in the village
of Shegar in central Tibet.

Throughout Tibet it is
possible to find street-side
pool tables in use.

A small monastery in the Amdo region of eastern Tibet.

Though the "cowboys" of eastern Tibet often ride horses, they are equally at home on yaks. As a rule, yaks are more high-strung and temperamental than domestic cattle.

The cattle drive is a common sight in many parts of Tibet. Whole families move their herds of yaks, goats, sheep, and horses many miles seeking greener pastures.

Lesha's Café.

Monks of Labrang Monastery
consider their options at a
local optical store.

Preceding pages: A group of locals pitch in to free
this stranded truck from knee-deep mud.

Children are the center of attention in Tibetan families. It is common to see children carried on the backs of their mothers and siblings. Older children help care for their younger brothers and sisters.

A nomadic family waves farewell.

Preceding pages: The end of
another day near our camp on
the road to Gomang Monastery
in eastern Tibet.

A nomadic herdsman
comforts an orphaned lamb.
The mother of this newborn
died during the night, and it
will now be up to this young
boy to raise the lamb.

A girl enjoys a picnic near her family's remote farmstead in the grass-covered mountains of eastern Tibet.

A woman wearing the typical, everyday clothing and jewelry displayed by many Tibetans of the eastern regions. The jewelry is made from many different materials, including turquoise, coral, amber, bone, and silver. The silver hooks hanging on her belt are both ornamental and practical: they are sometimes used while milking the female yaks, or *dri,* to keep the milk pails from being kicked over.

A day laborer carries a stone to be used
in rebuilding a little-known monastery in
eastern Tibet.

138